Tell God How You Feel

christina Fox

Illustrated
by
Lisa
Flanagan

Children are often unsure about what to do with their emotions. Whether they are feeling happy or sad, peaceful or anxious, angry or joyful, they can learn healthy ways to share their emotions with God. Christina Fox's new book, *Tell God How You Feel* is a wonderful book to help parents and children discuss their feelings, as they consider the ways people have prayerfully talked to God all throughout Scripture, especially in the Psalms. This book is a wonderful way to talk with your children as you help them learn to talk to God.

Melissa Kruger
Author and Director of Women's Initiatives
for The Gospel Coalition

To my nieces
—Natalie and Bella—
May you always know
that God hears you
when you pray

Copyright © 2021 Christina Fox
ISBN 978-1-5271-0616-1

First published in 2021 and reprinted in 2021
by Christian Focus Publications
Geanies House, Fearn, Ross-shire, IV20 1TW
Scotland, U.K.
www.christianfocus.com

Illustrations by Lisa Flanagan
Cover design by Daniel van Straaten
Printed and bound by Bell and Bain, Glasgow

CONTENTS

Dear Parents,

This book is designed to help you engage your child/children on the topic of emotions, and more specifically, difficult emotions.

We are emotional beings. Created in the image of God, we reflect God; we mirror him in this world. One of the ways we do that is in our emotions. God feels emotions such as love, joy, peace, jealousy, anger, and sadness (Exodus. 34:14, Romans. 1:18, Romans. 5:5, John 11:35). When we feel joy and gladness at the goodness of God, we image him. When we feel righteous anger at the effects of sin in the world, we reflect God.

But unlike God, our emotions are not holy and perfect. Like all things, sin has impacted our emotions. The impact of the Fall brought on by our first parents' sin is felt far and wide. Bad things happen. People get sick and die and we mourn their loss. People hurt and abuse us. Frightening things happen in the world around us—disasters, plagues, violence, job loss, divorce, and more. We hurt others with our selfishness. All of these situations are the result of sin and they all produce emotional responses within us. Sometimes we respond in sinful ways to the pains of life. Often, our emotions will cloud the truth, exaggerate the truth, or distort the truth.

That is why developing the spiritual discipline of turning to God's Word to shine the light of truth into our circumstances is so important. *Tell God How You Feel* helps children learn that God's Word is our source of hope when our emotions take us on a roller coaster ride. When we are fearful, hurt, sad, and lost, God's Word is the anchor that keeps us secure.

The Psalms of Lament:

If you are unfamiliar with the Psalms of Lament, there are a few things you should know to help you as you teach your children about the Psalms. First, the book of Psalms is the Bible's hymn book. The Israelites used the Psalms in their worship the way we sing our hymns and spiritual songs in church on Sunday mornings.

The book of Psalms contains many different genres of prose, written by different authors, including David, Moses, and Israel's worship leaders. The Psalms are not organized by type, but as you read them, you can tell that they are different. Some Psalms are praise songs, singing praises to God for his goodness and faithfulness. Some are songs of thanksgiving, thanking God for a specific deliverance. There are also dark Psalms called laments. These are the Psalms where the writer voices difficult and painful emotions. He tells God in vivid and descriptive words and metaphors that he is sad, afraid, or lonely, among other emotions.

The laments have a common pattern. They usually begin with the author describing their circumstances and how they feel about it. The author then asks God to help or to intervene in some way. At the end of the lament, the author often ends with words of praise and worship. It is this pattern we want our children to learn and implement in their own prayers to God.

children and their emotions:

1. Children need to learn to identify their emotions: Children don't automatically know that the tightness in their belly or the pounding of the heart means they are afraid. They need the words to describe it. It's important that we help our children gain a vocabulary for naming their emotions. You can help them by using words that describe emotions. You can describe your own emotions, "We are running late to our appointment and I'm worried we will miss it." "I am feeling frustrated because my computer isn't working today, and I can't get my work done." You can also point out to them when you identify their emotional responses, "You seem worried about your spelling test today." "I see that you are crying. Are you feeling sad because _____?"

2. Children don't always behave the way we expect: A child who is sad might not behave the way an adult does who is sad. Sometimes, increased psychomotor activity, distractedness, whining, and irritability are all indicators that a child is emotionally bothered by something. Emotions like fear, sadness, and loneliness can show up in strange ways. When your child is behaving differently than normal, consider what emotions might be lying beneath that behavior.

3. Emotions are part of what the Bible calls the "heart.": The Bible includes our emotions as part of a broader term, called the heart. When we read about the heart in the Bible it includes our thoughts, emotions, will, intention, choices, and beliefs. There is a strong relationship between our beliefs and emotions. What we believe and think shapes our emotions. That's why not everyone has the same emotional response to the same life circumstance. When we train our hearts through reading and studying God's Word, it transforms our thinking, which in turn will shape our emotions. This is why reading the Psalms helps us when we are going through a trial or difficult season. The Psalms remind us of what is true and in encountering the truth, we find our joy renewed.

4. Not only do we have a heart, but we also have a physical body. Our physical bodies impact our spiritual nature and vice versa. There is a complex relationship between the two. For example, we know how much stress impacts our physical health. When we consider our children's emotional responses, we have to remember this truth. Sometimes physical health problems can impact their emotions. We see this when they are tired or hungry. Medications can cause a change in emotions as well (For example, after a recent surgery, I woke up in the recovery room crying. I later learned it was a common side effect to anesthesia). As parents, we need to keep in mind the impact of our children's physical health on their emotions and seek medical help as needed.

5. Children need to know that emotions themselves aren't bad, it's how we respond to them that can be sinful: It's true, our emotions are not always an accurate indicator of reality. But they do tell us something is wrong. They reveal something in our heart. And while they aren't bad in and of themselves, we can respond to them in sinful ways. Feeling hurt and rejected by peers is a normal response to the unkindness of others, but it's not right to then turn and yell at a sibling. In helping our children learn to lament, they will learn a godly response

to their painful emotions. And as they mature (both in age and in spiritual wisdom), you can help your children learn to search their hearts and identify what thoughts, desires, and beliefs might be influencing their emotional responses.

6. Often, the ways we deal with our own emotions will come to the surface in response to our children's emotions. If we are uncomfortable with emotions, if we tend to stuff or hide what we are feeling, it will be difficult to help our children with their emotions. Here's the truth: we can't just tell a child, "Stop being sad" or "Stop being afraid." Rather, we need to help direct their emotions to the one who knows and cares about their tears. We need to help them see that God is their place of safety, their refuge to turn to when life hurts.

7. We all have a natural response to get rid of what hurts us. We want to hide from difficult or uncomfortable emotions, pretend they aren't there, or cover them up. As adults, we might eat a gallon of ice cream when we are stressed or upset. We might keep ourselves busy to distract us from what bothers us. Children might respond differently, but they still have a natural

tendency to want to protect themselves from uncomfortable emotions like fear and sadness. Be on the lookout for that. *Tell God How You Feel* is designed to help children learn to turn to God when they are upset.

8. An additional accompaniment to learning how to lament, is to help your children learn more about God's character. Take the time to study the names of God and his attributes with your children. Also study God's providence. These truths are ones that the psalmist turned to in his pain and sorrow and it's what our children need to do as well.

Ways to use this book:

1. Read it like you would any other picture book with your child. There are discussion questions at the end of each story which will help you engage your children about what they learned.

2. Read a particular story that relates to what your child is going through. If you know your child is dealing with fears about something, read Mia's story and talk to your child about what Mia learned about her fear.

3. Some of the discussion questions are designed for older elementary children and the rest are for younger children. Use the questions you think are best suited to your own child.

4. The stories chosen for this book are circumstances that most children will face in their childhood. Some children experience more painful and frightening situations than those in this book, such as abuse and severe loss. Even if your child has not experienced the exact circumstance as the child in the story, they still know what it's like to feel afraid, sad, rejected, or lonely. Use the discussion time to help them think through how they can relate to the emotions in the story, if not the exact scenario.

May this time with your children draw you closer to each other and to the Lord your refuge.

Christina Fox

A Scary Thunderstorm

Crash! Boom! Mia sprang up in her bed, her heart pounding.

Crash! Boom! There it was again.

Her room lit up like it was the middle of the day each time the skies pounded. Mia climbed out of bed and cracked open the blinds on her window.

Rain was pouring down, tapping at the glass. It sounded like when the letter carrier knocks on the door with a package.

Boom! Thunder banged right across the top of the house. The windows rattled. Then lightning cracked again. Mia's heart felt like it might jump right out her chest.

She sprinted down the hallway to her parents' room, jumped into their bed, and pulled the covers up over her face.

Mom felt Mia's legs trembling against hers and woke up.

"Mia, what are you doing here?" Mom asked.

"I'm scared," Mia whispered.

"Of the storm?" Mom asked.

Mia's head bobbed up and down beneath the covers.

By then Dad had woken as well. Mia cuddled up close between her parents.

"Since we're all awake, how about I tell you a story," Dad said.

"Ok," Mia responded.

Dad picked up his Bible from the nightstand and opened to 1 Samuel 19. He read the story of when King Saul was jealous of David because of his success in battle against Israel's enemies. Dad said, "Not only was David a mighty warrior, but he also played musical instruments. One day he was playing music for King Saul and Saul got so angry at David that he tried to kill him. David ran off before he could. Saul sent his men after David to kill him. David had to run for his life after that, sleeping in caves and relying on friends and family to sneak him food."

Dad looked at Mia. "What do you think David felt when Saul was angry at him and tried to hurt him?"

"Scared?" Mia guessed.

"You bet he was," Dad said. "Let me tell you just how scared he was." Dad then flipped in his Bible over to the book of Psalms.

"David wrote many Psalms in his life. He wrote a few of them when he was scared. Do you know what the Psalms are?" asked Dad.

"A book of the Bible," answered Mia, jumping as another boom echoed throughout her parents' bedroom.

"Yes. The Psalms are a book of the Bible. They were actually the songs the Israelites sang in worship just like we sing our hymns and praise songs on Sunday mornings at church. These songs were all different. Some were happy songs, sung when God rescued the Israelite's from harm. Some were sad songs. Some were praise songs, singing about the goodness of God. And some were even songs about being scared, like you are right now."

Dad went on to read part of what David said in Psalm 56 and said, "David wrote this while he was on the run from King Saul and ran to the Philistines, hoping they would help him, but they threatened his life as well."

"Be gracious to me, O God, for man tramples on me; all day long an attacker oppresses me; my enemies trample on me all day long, for many attack me proudly. When I am afraid, I put my trust in you. In God, whose word I praise, in God I trust; I shall not be afraid. What can flesh do to me?" (verses 1-4)

"Mia, what do you notice about what David wrote?" Mom asked.

"He was really scared," Mia said.

"Yes. What else?" Mom asked.

"He trusted God," Mia remarked.

By that time, the thunder was farther away, and Mia's heartbeat had returned to normal.

Dad said to Mia, "It's okay to be afraid. We are all afraid at times. Even King David who fought the giant Goliath was afraid. God doesn't want us to be afraid on our own. He wants us to come to him with our fears and tell him all about it. He loves you and cares about you, Mia. So much so, he knows about every tear you cry."

"Let's all pray together, like David did," Mom said.

Mom, Dad, and Mia prayed together and then she returned to her room and crawled up into her bed. As she closed her eyes, she whispered, "Thank you, God, for watching over me tonight."

Questions for Discussion:

1. Have you ever felt scared about something? What does your body feel like when you are scared?

(Some examples might be: heart pounds, sweaty palms, stomach feels tight or nauseous, head hurts, etc.).

Dad and Mom: share about a time you felt scared.

2. Do you know that God wants you to come to him when you are scared? Why?

3. David asked God to help him in this Psalm. What are some things you can ask God to do when you are scared?

(Example answers might be: ask for protection, rescue, help, etc.).

4. David also reminded himself about who God is. What are some things you can remember about God when you are scared?

(Some examples might be: God is all-powerful, all-knowing, he saves us, he hears us, etc.).

5. For older children: Do you think Jesus ever felt anxious about anything? Read Luke 22:39-46. Jesus faced the most scary thing ever, the cross, so we wouldn't have to. Sin is our greatest enemy and Jesus defeated it through his perfect life and sacrificial death. Because he conquered our greatest fear, we can trust him to be with us in all our other fears.

6. Pray together about your child's fear, applying what they learned from this story.

A Friend Moves Away

Josh walks down the steps of the school bus and slowly trudges home from the bus stop. He opens the door to the house and finds his mom just pulling cookies out of the oven. His favorite.

"Hi, honey. How was school? Moms asks.

He drops his backpack on the floor and bypasses the yummy smell of chocolate chip cookies. He heads for his room, shutting the door behind him.

Mom sets her potholder down and looks curiously at the stairs.

"Josh?" she calls.

No answer. Concerned, she walks up to his room and finds him face down on his bed.

"Josh?" Mom sits on the edge of his bed and begins to rub his back. "Are you not feeling well?" she asks.

Josh flips over and Mom sees his long face. "No, I'm fine," he mutters.

"You don't look fine. You look...sad" she remarks.

He heaves a deep sigh. "I guess I kind of am sad. Jack told me today that his dad got a new job. He has to move far away. I'll never see him again." Josh tries to hold them in, but tears begin leaking out the sides of his eyes. He quickly wipes them away.

Mom grabs him in a big hug. "Oh, honey. I am so so sorry. Jack is your best friend. No wonder you are sad. You've known each other since preschool. Do you remember?"

"Yes," Josh attempts a slight smile. "We used to build train tracks during free play time in Miss Kelly's class."

"And you've been friends ever since," Mom commented.

"Scoot over." Mom sets Josh's pillows up so they both can sit up with their backs against the pillows.

Mom grabs Josh's Bible sitting on the nightstand and says, "You know, there were two friends in the Bible who were the very best of friends."

"Who?" Josh asks.

"Jonathan and David," Mom says.

Mom opens to 1 Samuel 18 and reads about Jonathan and David's friendship. She tells Josh how they made an agreement to be the best of friends with each other and as part of the agreement, Jonathan gave David some of his most prized things, including his bow.

"Like when I gave Jack my favorite car, the red one with the spoiler on the back," Josh remarks.

"Yes, just like that," said Mom. "Did you know," Mom adds, "David also felt sad, like you feel right now?"

"Did he feel like someone stomped on his chest? Like the worst thing in the world happened?" Josh asked.

"He sure did, Josh." Mom flipped over to Psalm 13.

"One time, David was so sad, he wrote a prayer to God, telling him he was sad every single day." She read from Psalm 13: "How long must I struggle with anguish in my soul, with sorrow in my heart every day?"

"I just found out Jack is moving today. But I bet I'll be sad every day forever now," Josh declared.

Mom smiled and wrapped her arm around him. "When we care for someone and they move away, it's right that we feel sad. It's normal to feel that way. It hurts." She shifted against the pillows and turned around to Josh. "Josh, God wants you to tell him that you are sad. He wants you to tell him how much you'll miss your friend. He even wants to hear your questions about it."

"Like, 'why does Jack have to move?' and 'why couldn't God make his dad stay here?'" Josh asked.

"Yes," Mom said.

Mom pointed to the Psalm in the Bible. Josh saw how short it was and looked at where she pointed.

"David also prayed about his trust in God. He talked about God's goodness and God's love for him. When hard things like this happen, Josh, we have to remember who God is. He is a good God. We can trust him with whatever he gives us. It may be hard. It may be sad. But we can trust he is doing something good. We don't know what that is right now, and we don't have to. We just need to trust him."

Mom squeezed Josh's hand. "I'm going to pray for you right now, then how about we call up Jack's mom and invite him over for cookies and milk?"

"Can we?" Josh asked, his face lighting up.

Mom prayed that God would help Josh with his sadness and that Josh would know that God is always with him and that he wants to hear from him. "Amen," they said in unison.

"And let's plan some fun things to do with Jack before he moves. What would be fun for you guys to do together?" Mom asked.

"Well ..." Josh then went on to share all their favorite things to do.

Questions for Discussion:

1. Have you ever felt sad like Josh?

What did it feel like? What were you sad about?

2. Mom or Dad: tell about a time you felt sad.

3. The Bible tells us God wants us to pray to him when we are sad. Have you ever done that? Why do you think God wants us to do that?

4. For younger children: Mom or Dad, talk with your children about how God is our Father and just like your children come to you when they are hurt about something, we are to come to God with all our hurts.

Talk about times when they came to you when they were sad and how you comforted them. God does the same with us.

5. For older children: Do you think it is hard to trust God when something hard happens, like Josh's friend moving away?

Mom or Dad, read Psalm 13 aloud to your children. Why do you think David trusted God when he was so sad?

6. Pray with your children and model for them how to pray about feeling sad. Ask God questions. Ask him to help comfort you in sadness. Pray about your trust in God because he is good and trustworthy. Praise him for who he is.

A Friend's Rejection

"Okay, everyone. Put your books away. It's time for lunch," announces Mrs. Banks.

Everyone grabs their lunch boxes to line up and head to the cafeteria.

Mia grabs hers and tries to get in line with her best friend, Emily, but there's already a crowd of girls with her. Mia heads to the back of the line.

When they arrive at the cafeteria, Mia searches for Emily and finds her already seated. But the spot next to her is taken. The new girl, Samantha, is in the seat Mia always sits in. Every day this year, Mia has sat there. But not today. She looks at Emily with a question on her face, but Emily merely shrugs and turns to Samantha and they start to laugh together.

Mia feels her face turning red as she slinks off to find a seat at the end of the row. She eats her lunch in silence.

Later in art class, Mia is working on a group collage project with several other girls. One of them, Leanne, starts to talk about a tea party she is going to at the weekend. A party at Samantha's house.

Leanne turns to Mia and asks, "What are you wearing to the party?"

Mia puts her head down and mumbles, "I'm not going."

"What?" Leanne asks.

Mia looks up and pastes a smile on her face, "I'm too busy this weekend. I can't go." Inside, she thinks, Why was everyone else invited but not me?

"Oh. Too bad. It's going to be fun." Leanne turns to the other girls and they take turns talking about what they will wear.

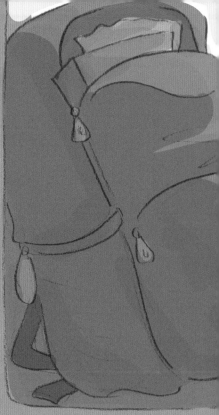

At the end of Art class, Mia stops and gathers her belongings to go home. She sees Emily and walks over to her.

"Emily," Mia says. Emily turns to look at her with a frown on her face.

"What?" she asks.

"Why didn't you save me a seat during lunch?" Mia asks.

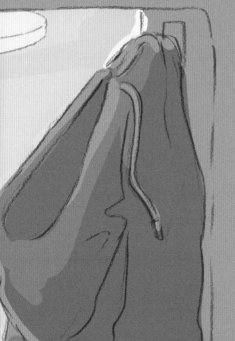

Emily shrugs and says, "Because I wanted to sit with Samantha. We're best friends now."

Mia feels her heart ache at Emily's words. She drops her head and stares at the floor. "But I thought we were best—"

Emily turns and sees Samantha headed toward her. "I have to go. I'm spending the night at her house so we can plan for the party this weekend."

Mom picks Mia up from school. As Mia opens the door to slide in the back seat, Mom looks at her in the rearview mirror and asks, "How was your day, sweetie?"

"Okay."

"Just okay?" Mom asks as she pulls into traffic. She drives down the road, expecting Mia to fill her in, but when she doesn't, she asks, "Mia, are you okay?"

Mia stares out the window of the back seat and a small tear falls down her face.

"No," she whispers.

Mom stops at a traffic light and turns around to look at her daughter.

"What is it?" she asks.

Mia sniffs and says in a rush, "Emily has a new best friend, a new girl to Fairburn Elementary. Her name is Samantha. Emily doesn't want to sit with me anymore. And Samantha is having a party and invited everyone but me!"

"I'm so sorry. You must be so hurt," Mom says.

Mia quietly cries the rest of the way home. Mom pulls the car into the garage and they walk into the kitchen together. Dad is there getting a drink from the refrigerator.

"Hey, Pumpkin! How was school today?" he asks.

Mia shrugs, her face red and blotchy from crying.

Mom puts her arm around Mia and says, "She's had a rough day. How about we go sit on the couch and talk about it?

Mia curls up between Dad and Mom on the couch and recounts to Dad what she already told Mom.

"Emily doesn't want to be my friend anymore!"

Dad says, "I am so sorry that happened to you, Mia. Being rejected by a friend hurts a lot, doesn't it?"

The family Bible is sitting on the coffee table. Dad opens it to the book of Psalms. "Did you know King David was hurt by a friend too?" Dad asked.

"No," Mia sniffed.

"He was so sad, he wrote a poem, called a Psalm." Dad flipped to Psalm 55 and read aloud, "For it is not an enemy who taunts me—then I could bear it; it is not an adversary who deals insolently with me—then I could hide from him. But it is you, a man, my equal, my companion, my familiar friend" (verses 12-13).

Dad turns to Mia and says, "David was hurt by a very dear friend. He's saying that kind of hurt feels worse than being hurt by someone who is not a friend."

"Yes!" Mia says. "I've known Emily since we were babies in the church nursery. It hurts so much that she doesn't like me anymore."

Mom pats Mia on the knee and remarks, "You know who else was hurt by his friends? Jesus. He knows what it feels like to be rejected by friends. When he needed his friends most, they all ran away from him. When he was taken to trial, his closest friend, Peter, denied knowing him."

"I remember my Sunday School teacher talking about that last Easter," Mia remarked.

Mia turns to Dad and asks, "Why do people hurt one another so much? Why do friends just decide not to like one another?"

Dad responds, "Because of sin, Mia. We hurt one another because we are sinners. That's why Jesus came to rescue us from sin. To make us into new people who love God and love one another instead of hurting one another."

"Mia," Mom says, "God wants you to tell him how hurt you feel by the way Emily treated you. Just like David prayed this prayer in Psalm 55, God wants you to pray and tell him how you feel. It says in this Psalm that God hears us and saves us."

"When our friends hurt us, Mia, we have a perfect friend in Jesus. He always loves us and will never reject us," Dad added.

"Never?" Mia asked. "Even if I mess up?"

"Yes. He is a friend who will never leave you," Mom said.

"How about you pray to him right now?" Dad asks.

"Ok, will you help?" Mia asked.

"Of course!" Dad agrees.

Mia bows her head and folds her hands. "Dear Jesus, I am so sad today because it feels like I've lost my best friend in the whole world. I feel so hurt that Emily has a new friend and doesn't want to be mine anymore. Mom says you hear me when I pray, please hear me." She peeks open her eyes and asks, "Can you finish, Dad?"

Dad nods and finishes her prayer, praying that Mia would know Jesus is her perfect friend and that he loves her. He prayed that Mia would be able to forgive her friend's unkindness, just as Jesus forgives her for her sin. He prayed that the Lord would help her to be a friend to someone else who might need a friend.

Then Dad and Mom give Mia a big hug.

Questions for Discussion:

1. Have you ever been hurt by a friend?

What happened?

How did you feel?

Mom and Dad: share about a time you were hurt by a friend.

How did you feel?

2. Why are friends so important to us?

Why does it hurt when they are unkind?

How do you react when a friend is hurtful?
(Cry, get angry, want to be mean back to them, etc.)

3. What makes a good friend?

Why is Jesus our perfect friend?

4. Is there someone you can think of who might need a friend right now?

How can you be a friend to that person?

5. For older children, read Luke 22:54-62.

How did Peter respond when people asked him if he knew Jesus?

Why do you think he responded that way?

What did Peter do when the rooster crowed a third time?

For further discussion, talk about how Jesus restored their friendship in John 21.

6. Parents, pray with your child/children. Help them to pray to God and tell him how their friendship hurts. Ask the Lord to heal their heart.

Feeling Lonely

Monday morning, Josh climbs the steps of the school bus and heads to his normal seat, three rows behind the bus driver. He sits alone. His best friend, Jack, moved away over the weekend.

He trudges through the school day and tries not to think about how much he misses his friend, but everywhere he turns, he remembers something funny his friend said or did.

In Science class, when the teacher spilled coffee on the front of his shirt and tried to wipe it off with his tie, he found himself turning behind him to look at Jack and share a laugh, but he wasn't there. During lunch, he sat with some of his other friends and talked about a movie coming out in the theater later this week. He had some laughs, but it just wasn't the same without Jack sitting beside him, swapping and sharing food out of their lunches.

At the end of the day, Josh climbed back up the stairs of the school bus and sat in his usual seat for the ride home. He wondered how he would get through the rest of the school year without his friend.

After dinner, Dad finds Josh in the living room, playing a video game. A racing game. The one he and Jack always played together when Jack came over.

"Josh," Dad said, "how's it going?" He walks over and puts a hand on his shoulder. "How's the game?"

"Fine," Josh mumbles.

"You doing okay?" Dad asks.

"I guess."

"Isn't this the game you and Jack always play?" Dad commented.

"Yes," Josh sighed. "It's just not as fun without him." He set the controller down and plopped back on the couch.

"I can imagine," Dad said. "It's hard when a friend moves away. Especially such a good friend. You must feel lonely without him."

Josh looked at Dad and lowered his eyes, a frown on his face. "I do. Nothing's the same. School wasn't fun without him to laugh with. And he won't be here to go to the movie with this weekend."

Dad scooted over on the couch and gave Josh a hug. "I'm sorry you are so lonely. Have you told God how you feel?"

Josh shrugged. "Not really. Doesn't he already know?"

"It's true, he does know how you feel. But he also wants you to tell him about it. To ask him to help you with those feelings," Dad said.

Dad picked up his Bible and remarked, "Remember how we've been reading some of King David's Psalms where he told God how he was feeling?"

"Yes."

"In one of those Psalms, Psalm 142, David was all alone. He was trapped in a cave, far away from his friends and family. He felt so alone, he thought no one cared about him at all." Dad read a verse, "I look for someone to come and help me, but no one gives me a passing thought! No one will help me; no one cares a bit what happens to me," (verse 4).

"Wow, he really does feel lonely," Josh remarked.

Dad asked, "But was he truly all alone?"

"Well, not really. God was with him," Josh said.

"That's right. God is always with us. Here's what David wrote in verse five, "Then I pray to you, O LORD. I say, 'You are my place of refuge. You are all I really want in life'." Dad pointed to the Psalm and said, "Josh, no matter how alone you are, God is your place of safety. He always hears you. He's always with you."

"I know God is with me, Dad. I just wish Jack was with me too," Josh said.

Dad hugged Josh again. "That's what you need to tell God when you pray. Tell him how hard it was at school today. Tell him how lonely you feel. Ask him to be your safe place. Ask him to give you hope, as David did in verse seven, 'Bring me out of prison so I can thank you. The godly will crowd around me, for you are good to me.' He's saying he wants to leave his cave and not be alone anymore. David is trusting in God's goodness. You can too."

"Being lonely today felt like being in a cave," Josh commented. "Do you think it will get better?" he asked.

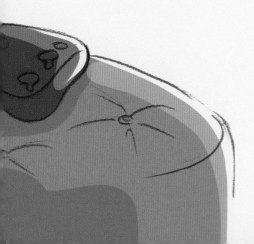

"It will, slowly. But no matter what, God is always your friend. You are never truly alone because Jesus' Spirit is with you. When you came to faith and believed in what Jesus did for you on the cross, he gave you his Spirit to live within you. The Spirit is also called our Comforter. He helps us when we need encouragement," Dad responded.

"I guess I never thought about the Holy Spirit being with me like that," Josh said.

"How about we pray together?" Dad asked.

Josh and Dad prayed together, taking turns. Josh told God that he felt lonely and missed Jack. He asked for help to not feel so alone at school. Dad prayed for Josh's heart, that the Spirit would encourage him and comfort him. He prayed that God would be a refuge for Josh.

"Now what's this I hear about a new movie coming out this weekend?" Dad asked.

"It's going to be awesome!" Josh exclaimed and then went on to explain.

"How about we go together? Just the two of us guys?" Dad suggested.

Josh smiled. "Can we get popcorn and candy?"

"You bet!" Dad agreed. "And afterward, why don't you call Jack and you two can talk about it?"

"I will!" Josh said.

Questions for Discussion:

1. God made us to be connected to other people in friendship. That's why we feel lonely when we aren't near our friends.

What does it feel like when you are lonely?

Dad and Mom: share about a time you felt that way.

2. Why should we tell God about our feelings if he already knows?

Why did David pray to God when he was in the cave?

3. With your older children, read Psalm 142 and talk about how David describes what he is feeling.

Look at how he described God. While the Psalm starts out with a sad tone, how does it end?

Why does David end it that way?

4. Talk about what a refuge is.

How can God be our refuge when we are feeling lonely?

5. Before Jesus left, he told his friends it was good that he was leaving them. That must have been hard for them to understand. They must have wondered why it would be good for him to leave. Surely, they would miss him! Jesus explained why in John 14:16.

Talk with your children about the Holy Spirit and his role as Comforter.

6. Pray with your children about their loneliness. Help them to tell God how they feel.

Thankful for a Good Grade

Josh rushed through the back door, shoving it aside with a loud whoosh. He ran into the kitchen calling out as he went:

"Mom! Mom!" he yelled. "Guess what I got on my spelling test?"

Mom stood up from her crouched position on the floor where she was tidying up the bottom of the pantry. She turned toward Josh as he skidded to a halt in front of her, holding out a piece of paper he waved up and down.

"Guess!" he repeated.

"An 'A'?" she asked.

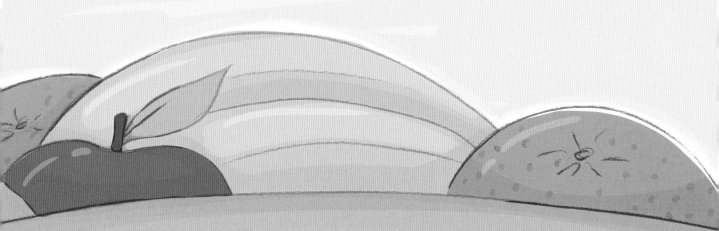

"Not just an "A," Josh announced, with a wide grin, "I got a hundred!"

"That's fantastic!" Mom hugged him tight. "All that time you spent practicing your words paid off."

Josh climbed up on the stool at the breakfast bar and grabbed a snack from the bowl.

"Can we do something to celebrate when Dad gets home later?" Josh asked.

Mom walked over to the fridge and poured Josh a cup of milk.

"I'm sure Dad will be excited to hear your good news. Let's talk about how to celebrate during dinner tonight."

Josh downed his milk and hopped off the stool. "Ok, Mom!"

Just as fast as he ran into the house, he quickly ran out the door to ride his bike around the cul-de-sac.

Later that evening, Dad walked through the door as Josh and Mia were helping set the table for dinner.

Josh looked up and smiled at his dad.

"You'll never guess how I did on my spelling test today, Dad."

"Hmm. Let's see," Dad said, "you got two wrong?"

"Nope. Guess again." Josh challenged.

"Five wrong?" Dad teased.

"No! I got ZERO wrong!"

Dad fist pumped Josh as they all sat down at the dinner table.

Mom asked, "Whose turn is it to pray tonight?"

Dad said, "I think Josh should. He has a lot to be thankful for."

He turned to Josh, "Why don't you thank God for your good grade in spelling today?"

"Really?" asked Josh, "God cares about things like that?"

"He certainly does," Dad answered.

Mom remarked, "Remember how we've talked about the book of Psalms the last few weeks?"

Josh nodded.

"Well, the men who wrote the Psalms didn't just tell God when they were sad or worried or scared. They also told God when they felt grateful. In fact, everything we have comes from God so it's only right that we give him thanks," Mom said.

Dad opened the Bible that always sat in the center of the dining table. Flipping half-way through the book, he found a verse and read it. "I will praise you, O LORD, with all my heart; I will tell of all your wonders. I will be glad and rejoice in you; I will sing praise to your name, O Most High" (Psalm 9:1-2).

"Josh, God is the giver of all good things and he deserves our thanksgiving and praise," Dad said.

"So, he wants us to thank him for both big things and small things?" Josh asked.

"Yes," Mom answered. "What are some things you are grateful for that you can give him thanks for?"

Josh thought. "Well, I'm thankful for our dog, Charlie. And for the fishing trip we went on last weekend. That we get to see Grandma next week when she comes for a visit. Oh, and those brownies you made the other day."

Mia wanted to share things too. "I want to thank God for my new bike I got for my birthday. Also, for the new friend I made in school this week. And, for the break we get from school next week," she said with a smile.

Before long, everyone was saying what they were thankful for. It was like a volleyball game, each person going back and forth with something good God had done for them.

They went on so long that Mia touched the food on her plate and remarked, "Uh, Josh, our food is getting cold. Maybe you should pray now?"

Everyone laughed and then bowed their heads, grabbing each other's hands.

Josh prayed, "Father, thank you so much for helping me remember how to spell my words today. I didn't think I'd ever get better in spelling, much less make an "A." Thank you for all you do for us. There's so much we could thank you for and if we did, we'd never get to eat our dinner! Oh, and thank you for our food. In Jesus' name, Amen."

Questions for Discussion:

1. Have you ever been grateful for something, like Josh was for his good grade?

Tell us about that time.

Parents share too!

2. Do you think God wants to hear from you about those good things that happened?

Why?

3. In the Psalm Josh's Dad read, the writer of the Psalm mentioned telling of God's wonders.

What does that mean?

Do you ever tell others of the things God has done for you?

4. Take turns sharing things you are thankful for that God has done.

5. In addition to thanking God for all the things he gives us, we should also thank him for the biggest thing he has given us: his Son, Jesus Christ.

Why should we be thankful for Jesus?

6. Pray a prayer together, thanking God for what he's done, both the big and little things.

CHRISTIAN FOCUS PUBLICATIONS

Christian Focus | **Christian Heritage** | **CF4K** | **Mentor**

Christian Focus Publications publishes books for adults and children under its four main imprints: Christian Focus, CF4K, Mentor and Christian Heritage. Our books reflect our conviction that God's Word is reliable and Jesus is the way to know him, and live for ever with him.

Our children's publication list includes a Sunday School curriculum that covers pre-school to early teens, and puzzle and activity books. We also publish personal and family devotional titles, biographies and inspirational stories that children will love.

If you are looking for quality Bible teaching for children then we have an excellent range of Bible stories and age-specific theological books.

From pre-school board books to teenage apologetics, we have it covered!

Find us at our web page: www.christianfocus.com

CF4•K
Because you're never
too young to know Jesus